Artificial
Beauté

Artificial
Beauté
THE BREAKTHROUGH

Six Stories of Transforming from Hurt to Healing

BONITA PARKER

purposely created
PUBLISHING

ARTIFICIAL BEAUTÉ: THE BREAKTHROUGH

Published by Purposely Created Publishing Group™

Copyright © 2017 Bonita Parker

All rights reserved.

No part of this book may be reproduced, distributed or transmitted in any form by any means, graphics, electronics, or mechanical, including photocopy, recording, taping, or by any information storage or retrieval system, without permission in writing from the publisher, except in the case of reprints in the context of reviews, quotes, or references.

Unless otherwise indicated, scripture quotations are from the Holy Bible, King James Version. All rights reserved.

Scriptures marked NLT are taken from the New Living Translation®. Copyright © 1996, 2004, 2007, 2013 by Tyndale House Foundation. All rights reserved.

Printed in the United States of America

ISBN: 978-1-947054-02-8

Special discounts are available on bulk quantity purchases by book clubs, associations and special interest groups. For details email:
sales@publishyourgift.com
or call (888) 949-6228.

For information logon to:
www.PublishYourGift.com

Dedication

For this book, I give thanks and dedicate it to the Almighty for His gracious mercy, healing, and deliverance of all the women who contributed to this anthology. *Without you, we fail your divine assignment, ourselves, and, most of all, the community that we are here to serve.*

Bonita

Table of Contents

Foreword ix

Introduction xi

Invisible Colors
by Bonita Parker 1

Who Am I?
by Ida Robinson 19

Breaking Down the Scaffold
by Anne Sewell 33

Who's Cheating Who?
by LuDrean Peterson 49

Pain Producing Purpose
by Kimberly Moorer 63

More Than a Conqueror
by Elecia James 77

About the Authors 89

Foreword

Artificial Beauté: The Breakthrough, compiled by Inner Beauté Synergist and transformation coach, Bonita Parker, alongside five courageous women who also share their stories, is an inspiring written work that will remind you of the freedom you can experience when you make a conscious decision to unmask your hidden struggles, tell your raw and authentic truth, expose your dysfunction, and freely forgive. The stories in this book are stories of courage, willpower, discovery, self-evaluation, and the power to overcome obstacles and challenges that threaten to steal your joy in life.

As you immerse yourself in each story, you will feel energized to tap into your own ability to soar beyond the things that unexpectedly knock you down. You will undoubtedly begin to reflect on your own life and start to peel back your own layers of hurt, discouragement, failures, disappointment, and dysfunction. But as you peel back those layers, you will also emerge with a renewed sense of commitment to intentionally steering your life in the direction you choose. Each story in *Artificial Beauté: The Breakthrough* will leave you feeling inspired, empowered, and reassured that if these women have risen out of the ashes like a phoenix, so can you.

As a Global Women's Empowerment Champion

on a mission to empower and equip women to walk in their greatness without regrets, I endorse this book as an impactful read and as a tool that will propel beyond what has happened to you in order to discover what is waiting for you. *Artificial Beauté: The Breakthrough* will equip you to claim personal power over your past, your present, and your future.

As you allow the powerful words from each author in this book to penetrate, remind yourself daily that you have everything it takes to overcome any obstacle and come out a victor! Nothing can stop you unless you give it permission. Be sure to keep a copy of this book close at hand to refer to as a resource that will prompt you to continue assessing where you are in your journey and to determine how you can become the very best version of yourself.

After reading this book, I am confident that you will develop the tenacity to plow through the setbacks, obstacles, challenges, and fears you presently face. I believe you will become bolder as you claim what you want out of life, and then audaciously go out and get it. Rest assured that you will feel stronger than ever before and you will position yourself to show the world what you are truly made of!

Cheryl Wood
International Keynote Speaker & Speaker Development Coach
www.CherylWoodEmpowers.com

Introduction

When we are faced with adversity and real-life trauma, we can react in two ways—either by losing all hope and falling into self-destructive habits, or by using the challenge to find our inner strength.

The truth of the matter is, we are all much stronger than we believe ourselves to be, and the discovery of our inner strength and determination will surface most often when we are faced with adversity.

The raw, very riveting stories in this anthology will inspire you to overcome your own challenges, encourage you to face your fears, and battle the invisible enemies that have held you in a place of captivity, controlled your thoughts, and limited your beliefs. Now is the time to remove all self-doubt, increase your self-confidence, and unmask yourself.

The empowering and uplifting stories by these women—who have overcome some very real challenges, honed in on their inner strength, and changed their lives—will help you find your internal happiness, peace, and resilience, and remind you that all things are possible when you dig deep and tap into the power that you have within you.

When I decided to open up the opportunity to

women who wanted a platform to pour into others and share their personal power stories, I went in with the intent of selecting those who I could personally resonate with due to my own internal battles and life struggles. I was in no way prepared for the emotional awakening that occurred as I began reading and editing the stories that you are about to read. I was deeply moved by the strong will and determination demonstrated by the contributors of this book. *They were fearless beyond measure.*

Their stories will make you laugh and make you cry; some may anger you, but all of them will, beyond a doubt, make you realize that inside of you lies your own strength, your own fearlessness, and your own determination needed to overcome any obstacle that stands in your way, or any challenge that is still harboring your breakthrough. Your best life is waiting on the other side of the personal power story inside of you. You just have to get it out and share it with the world, just as these women are sharing with you. *We want your breakthrough.*

In chapter 1, you'll read about owning your truth, being transparent, and learning the art of forgiveness as I, Bonita Parker—certified life coach and transformation strategist and the visionary and author of the Artificial Beauté anthology series—share my personal triumphs surrounding childhood abandonment by my maternal parent and the suffering effects that it unknowingly had on me as I moved throughout life. I reveal to you how this childhood trauma hindered my relationships with women, including my own blood sisters, and affected my ability to bond with my daughter. You will see how the power of God moved in me in such a way that forced me to deal with my truth head on as I was stripped of my mask, broken down into my most transparent state, and transformed into my best self—unapologetically and authentically.

In chapter 2, you will read about Ida Robinson's struggle as a single, teenage mother who was simply the product of her environment. Ida is a motivational speaker and author who speaks of her determination to go against the odds and how she used the stereotypes of young African American teen moms to serve as her strength as she continued her mission to graduate from high school. Her story will empower you to attack your goals with fervor and not let anything stand in your way, no matter what the obstacles may be. With the will to succeed, you can accomplish anything.

Chapter 3 will send you through a myriad of emotions as Anne Sewell, CEO of Creative Vision for Women, takes you through her whirlwind story of mental, physical, and sexual abuse. She shares with you the lowest points of her life that for many years held her hostage in a place of hurt and anger, disappointment and fear, and most of all, helplessness and self-destruction. She had all but given up on herself until she was put in a position to choose her life over everything—and everyone—and was confronted with having to forgive the person who changed her life in every single aspect.

In chapter 4, you are guided through one woman's refusal to forgive and the turmoil that it had on her life. Cheating her way through life and using non-forgiveness as her ultimate defense mechanism, LuDrean Peterson, CEO and founder of Delivering On Ideas & Thoughts (DOIT!), journeys with you as she relives the childhood trauma that stemmed from her father's absence from her life, and the negative choices that accompanied her lack. Having adopted a "get them before they get me" attitude, she shares with you how her life was heavily impacted and filled with distrust and disdain for anyone who tried to see her true heart.

Chapter 5 tells the tale of how looking for love in the wrong places can feel so right. Kimberly Moorer, motivational speaker and mentor, is a Christian woman who had a very simple dream: to have a loving husband, a family, and to live happily ever after. Her dreams were shattered when she learns of the reality of her husband's infidelity, and her perspective of what love and relationships should look like drastically changed right before her eyes. Putting God on the forefront of her union, she was positioned to forgive him—but at a cost. Her self-esteem was shattered, her confidence was compromised, her trust was jeopardized, and her faith had been tested to what seemed like its point of no return, but she pushed her way through it and continued to serve from her heart and not her hurt.

Artificial Beauté

Our final chapter, a powerful story written by Elecia James, challenges your belief in true sisterhood and the bond that siblings should share. She grew up with her worst enemy living under the same roof, sleeping only footsteps away. Elecia shares with you how mental abuse reared its ugly head by way of her sister and filled her up with fear, self-doubt, limiting beliefs, and a spirit of loneliness and confusion. After some years of separation, just when Elecia thought she had some reprieve, her father fell ill, and she was forced to confront her sister and again restore her faith in forgiveness.

The uniqueness of these stories is that they are real, raw, and uncut. These contributors had to dig deep; some had to relive the trauma and endure the lasting effects of what they've gone through. So if you read a story that resonates with you or even reminds you of someone else who you believe could benefit from the message in the story, please do not hesitate to share. Remember, our story is not for us; it's for the many people who need to know that they are not alone; that someone else has been through the same thing that they have gone through; that they have someone to laugh and cry with and, more importantly, someone who they can call a sister-friend. If for some reason you find yourself wanting to connect on a more personal level with the contributors, be sure to read their bio at the end of the book where they have also provided their contact information.

I hope you enjoy reading this book as much as we

did sharing with you. Our wish is that it impacts your life the way that it has mine, the contributors,' and so many women who may already be familiar with our personal power stories.

Changing lives one mask at a time…
Your sister in peace and prosperity,

Bonita Parker
INNER BEAUTE' SYNERGIST

INVISIBLE COLORS

One Woman's Hidden Truth

Written by
Bonita Parker

I'd much rather be honest and authentic and disappoint some people, than to exhaust myself trying to keep up the façade of perfection.

I used to tell myself that I was "just a girl who was very different from everyone else." I did not realize at the time that *that* was my own rendition of the truth—my truth. The fact remains that I was indeed just like so many women out here trying to make it in the crazy, judgmental world we live in. The difference between them and me was that I wore my colored mask better than most. And by my own choice.

It was a hot, humid day in June 1978. I was a five-year-old girl living in a world that was entirely too small for my outgoing personality. Decked out in my favorite yellow sundress and flip-flops with my two French braids on top of my head, I thought I was cute. I was super excited and anxious to see what Daddy had in store for us to do that evening when he got home. Spending the day with my uncle and 'nem wasn't exactly my idea of fun. I would have preferred role-playing with my dolls until Daddy came home—unlike my sisters. You see, I'm the youngest of three, with two older sisters who had their own idea of what interested them, and playing dolls with me was not one of them.

Every Friday, we were afforded the luxury of eating out, however, this day was slightly different. Upon entering our cozy two-bedroom apartment, Daddy told us to come sit down at the dining room table—he needed to talk to us. Now, in my household, the dining room table was where all of our family meetings and disciplinary discussions took place, so naturally, my sisters and I were all on edge thinking that we were in some kind of trouble. As Daddy began to talk, the more words that came out of his mouth, the more my heart sank deeper down inside my chest. The man who I had only been living with for a short while was now gently telling me that we would be going away for a little while—without him—to a place called North Carolina. That was where my family lived, he said. And they were going to assist him with taking care of me and my sisters while he took care of some things to prepare for us coming to live with him permanently.

Just to give you a little background, I am a woman who was left behind as a small child by her mother. I use the term "left behind" because "abandoned" seems so harsh—but I guess we *are* dealing with a harsh reality here, right? Simply put, I was abandoned by a woman who, at the time, decided that she was not ready for the stresses that came along with motherhood. Sound familiar to anyone? No one is ever *truly* ready for parenting, but society says you learn as you go, and you take the good with the bad and make it work, right? Hmmm. Nevertheless, I sat in front of the nice old Caucasian lady who would periodically babysit us, wondering when my mother would be coming back to pick us up. Wondering, how long does it take to go to the store? And what could she possibly be getting that would take so long? Minutes would turn into hours. Hours would turn into days. And right before my innocent eyes, my life as I had known it had drastically changed.

I will tell you that I do not recall how I actually felt in that particular moment, but what I do know is that it did affect me—only, at that time, I was clueless as to how. What I do remember vividly was my dad arriving to pick my sisters and me up to come live with him. He never uttered a negative word about my mother, but I can only imagine that her decision had disrupted his soul—even if just a little bit—for life as he knew it was about to change drastically as well. He went from a bachelor to a single father with three young girls—ages five, seven, and eight—to raise on his own, without any notice. The beauty in that was that he did so with no complaints, no hesitation, no fight. He stepped up to the plate and rose to the occasion as I imagine any father who truly loves his kids would do.

Back to that day in July. I stood in the doorway watching as Daddy packed up our belongings and began loading up the yellow Datsun pick-up truck that we all cozied up in every time we went somewhere. There was only a short time left before we'd be hitting the road at the crack of dawn and heading to North Carolina. I asked him why we had to leave and if we had made him mad. As a child, it's natural for you to feel like you did something wrong whenever your parents make drastic, life-changing decisions.

Artificial Beauté

He responded, "No. You all did nothing wrong." There was a look of sadness in his eyes.

The ride down was very peaceful. I don't recall any talking going on, just an occasional sound from the radio, a pit stop to the gas station, and another to the rest stop to use the bathroom. The next thing I knew, we were in North Carolina. Tons of family awaited us, including my grandma, who would be our primary caretaker. She was the epitome of a strong black woman with a very nurturing spirit. She made sure to shower us with love and make us feel very welcomed. For the first time in my life, I knew how it felt to be part of a family. Big Sunday dinners after church became the norm; and my grandmother instilled in us at a very early age how to conduct ourselves as true southern belles: very self-sufficient, respectable young women.

The next few years of my life went by extremely fast, but true to his promise, after a couple of years, Daddy came back for us. But I was in no way the same little girl that he had dropped off in the country that hot summer day in 1978. We loaded up and headed back to Maryland to a nicer apartment, with our own beds and dressers. I was eight years old and had learned and mastered the art of masking and pretending to be someone else.

When I lived in North Carolina, my cousins and I would often play house, pretending to be adults; we would play school, pretending to be teachers or students in high school; and we would play "church," pretending to be some of the people who attended our local church. I found it intriguing because, under the surface, it gave me the opportunity to be someone else—someone who others couldn't actually see; someone who others didn't actually know. And subconsciously, I carried this trait with me from that point forward. I had begun to build my wall of protection so that anybody who attempted to invade my up-close and personal space would not be able to penetrate my emotional core.

Years went by and one of the girls at school asked me, "Where is your mother? I've never seen her and you never talk about her."

The question stopped me dead in my tracks and threw a World Series curveball at me. So many emotions ran through my mind in that moment, and the only response that I could muster up was, "She's dead."

That was the first response that came to my mind. And because she was not present in my life, and I had no idea where she was, I had ultimately convinced myself that she was indeed dead. It became easier to pretend she was dead each time I said it out loud. Hell, it was definitely much easier to tell people that lie versus having a long discussion explaining why or how she abandoned me; how she did not want me; how she left me believing that she would come back for me; how she obviously did not love me—*me*—the real me, the innocent version of me, the little ole me who simply wanted, needed, and longed for a mother–daughter conversation that I knew would never come. Internally,

Artificial Beauté

I grieved for a relationship with her, but on the surface, this is how I learned to cope with her absence.

They say that once you tell one lie, you have to keep up the façade and tell more lies to cover up the first one.

Once I entered high school, I was even more determined that no one else was going to hurt me or be positioned to disappoint me to the magnitude that it affected me at my core. I developed a front of self-confidence that saved me from being viewed as the "outcast," but instead, someone who others would envy and look up to. I gave off the impression of this supreme girly girl who was very prim and proper, always keeping my nails and hair done and wearing cute little dresses instead of the standard jeans and sneakers that all of the other girls were wearing. The girls at school were drawn to me because of who they believed me to be. On the surface, I had it going on and came across as a mature young woman who had it all together. And while I was very well liked as *this* person, I still made the very conscious decision to not let anyone get too close to me. Despite this, on the inside, I felt lonely and full of self-doubt. I know this was the remnant of the abandonment that I'd experienced from my mother's leaving.

Ironically enough, my senior year of high school

came with many surprises. I ended up getting pregnant by one of the most popular guys in high school. However, it was nothing that I was proud of or happy about. I had long since decided that I never wanted to have kids because I did not want to do to them what my mother had done to me. I did not know how to love anyone other than myself at the time, and I was still questioning whether I was capable of even that. But the fact was, I was pregnant, and this baby would need a mother who could love it, cherish it, and protect it by any means necessary. I did not know quite how to be a mother—how to love as a mother—but I knew what it should look like. I've seen love in other mother–daughter relationships, but what wasn't in me couldn't be displayed or delivered. So I pulled out the yellow pages and contacted an adoption agency.

We never realize how our actions and decisions affect another human being until we are stripped of our mask and forced to reveal ourselves.

Moving through life and entering into adulthood, women became my nemesis. Unbeknownst to them, I was very distrustful and held them in very low regard. In my mind, they were untrustworthy, selfish little liars who were incapable of being genuine. So I began treating them as such. I chose my associations very wisely, and each one had to serve a unique purpose that was beneficial to me. My motto became "guilty until proven innocent," and anyone who did not play by my rules was disposed of immediately. I made a vow to never allow them to see me—the real me. And I allowed them to think of me what they pleased. I was okay with that. As far as I was concerned, their thoughts and assumptions were not *my* problem.

Most thought that I was stuck up and bougie; therefore, I became that, even though I knew it was far from the truth. I warded women off if I felt they were trying to get too close to me or if they were digging too deep into my personal space—I wasn't having that. I was very cautious not to share certain aspects of my personal life or the things that had happened to me. And if someone asked questions, I would go right into my defense mode and shut them out by either finding a reason to cut off communication or sabotaging the relationship. That was the mentality that I adopted. I became the aggressor in all relationships and friendships that I entered into. This was something that I practiced even in my relationships with women in my family and my own blood sisters. I kept them at arms' length and did not trust them with personal aspects of my life. I believed that if I wasn't good enough in my authentic self to make my own mother want to stay in my life, how could I expect and believe that other women would stay if they knew the real me?

When some children are abandoned, specifically by their maternal parent, it's easy for them to wear the invisible protective gear and conclude that it's better to do the hurting and abandoning than to risk having someone else do it to you. But at some point, it will begin to cost you something.

After spending years of isolating everyone, by my thirty-fifth birthday, I started feeling different. I realized that I was getting older and was ready to settle down and have people around me with whom I could grow older. I decided it was time for me to get some help to move past the ill emotions that I was harboring and start healing from the lifetime of hurt.

That year, I met the woman who would ultimately change my entire life. She was a spiritual life coach. Initially, she sought me out to plan an event for her, but when our spirits did not connect, she pulled back and told me that I was not ready to work with her. And while it took me aback at first, I clearly understood her stance. I was still in that place of holding back from women. Nevertheless, we spoke again some months later, and she ended up becoming my mentor and spiritual advisor. Her tutelage is what led to my mental breakthrough and internal healing. I realized that the absence of my mother had hindered me over the years and halted my personal development—which was the catalyst that forced me to conceal my vulnerability and true identity.

Slowly but surely, I began repairing damaged relationships and opening up to women, realizing that those relationships were what was missing from my life. I was missing someone I could call a sister, a friend, and a confidant, and be truly genuine with. This mentoring also allowed me to get to know myself and grow full circle, especially as a parent. I began loving and embracing the woman I had become and I learned how to return that love—specifically with my own daughter, a relationship that had suffered while I was in my own state of torment. And while nothing could make up for the years I'd lost being the mother she deserved, this was the relationship that I valued the most and worked the hardest at mending. I made sure to let her know that she was not a mistake and that my decision at attempting to give her up for adoption many years ago was one that stemmed from the young, broken-spirited girl who simply did not know how to give maternal love. But I had grown into someone very different.

I became what I believed love should look like. I became the example—genuine and transparent.

One beautiful Sunday morning in October 2014, I was lying cuddled up in the arms of the man I love and my phone rang. I reached over and glanced at the caller ID, which simply said "North Carolina" along with the phone number. Naturally, I assumed it would be someone from my family calling, so I gladly answered the call. "Hello," I said.

And the voice on the other end—one that was unfamiliarly familiar to me—responded, "Hi baby, this is your mother."

I froze. The room suddenly got small. The space around me suddenly felt tight and closed in. I instantly felt sweltering hot on the inside, and that's when it happened. The phone fell to the floor, and the anxiety attack crept in with a vengeance. I could not breathe. And while tears fell like a river from my eyes, the screaming sounds inside of me would not escape my throat. My whole body was trembling, and I felt as if I had seen the ghost that lived inside of every woman with whom I came in contact with. My honey wrapped me in his arms and held me while coaching me into breathing. I managed to whisper, "It's her," and he knew without a shadow of a doubt who the "her" was. He knew the true story and how it affected me. He reached over and hung up the phone while comforting me, telling me it would be okay. Giving me that moment.

Hurt people, hurt people. I was tired of hurting and being angry, and tired of building my wall, protecting my layers, and wearing my mask. Anger is always the emotion that festers first when we are faced with adversity because it allows us the free space to hide the true emotions that lie beneath the surface. Are you really angry or are you hurt? Give yourself permission to explore those emotions and feel what you truly feel under the mask. Allow yourself to mourn in your most transparent form—guilt free—so that the healing can begin.

After the phone call, I reached out to my mentor for another session and shared with her what had transpired. Naturally, she coached me through that process, which was the final stage of my healing. I often wondered when the day would come when I would hear from my mother; I knew it would eventually. God has a way of testing our faith and growth, and this was the only thing left on the table. The only thing that I had not cleared the air on. To me, she was still dead—in a mental sense. Physically, I knew she was alive and kicking just from conversations with my dad. Not too long beforehand, he had explained to me that she wanted my phone number to reconnect with me. My stance was that too much time had passed and it was too late for her to be my mother. I was better off without her in my life. You see, in that moment, I realized that I was still holding on to the pain and hurt that had held me captive for so many years. I had forgiven her no more than I had gotten over the fact that she had left. I was mad with myself for allowing myself to still be affected by it. And while mentoring had allowed me to release the anger and resentment that I had toward her for leaving, I still knew in my heart that a relationship with her would never happen.

In April 2015, I got a call that my mother had passed away. I was void of tears, and as insensitive as it may sound, a sense of relief came over me. My lie became my truth. And I knew that the final stage to my healing was complete forgiveness. I never got the chance to find out her "why," but I took comfort in knowing that neither of us was positioned to suffer any longer. I attended the funeral with the intent on settling the debt I owed to myself and closing that chapter of my life.

As I entered the church, a wave of calm fell over me. I wasn't anxious or angry when I took my place on the front pew with my sisters. I felt no remorse or ill feelings as I looked over at the poster-sized picture of the woman who I resembled. And I respectfully accepted the condolences that were handed out as we waited for the eulogy to begin. And as it did, I listened intently to the stories and praise from people who knew, loved, and respected her. One in particular captured my attention: My aunt told the story of how my mother had followed my career as an entrepreneur and was so proud of me for writing my first book, of which she had purchased a copy. I was in awe. In that moment, I forgave myself for my decision to not get to know her. And I also knew that it was time to put this chapter of my life completely behind me so that I could be open to receiving all that life had to offer—and what GOD had called upon me to do.

Artificial Beauté

I stood over her casket with my eyes closed and told her, "I don't need to know why you left, but just know that I forgive you." And for the first time in my life, I felt my shoulders relax and took a long deep breath. When I exhaled, all of the mental anguish, hurt, and anger completely left my body. I felt free.

Forgiveness does not mean that you consent to the wrongdoings of others but rather make the determination to free yourself from the internal prison that holds you in bondage from moving forward. When you make the choice to forgive, not only are you allowing it permission to fester in your spirit, but you also become the servant of your own suffering. Forgiving and then letting go is the only answer, as you cannot control the choices other people make—only the ones you make. Choose forgiveness. When one truly loves herself, forgiving becomes necessary.

"You must forgive the people who hurt you so you can get out of prison. You'll never be free until you do. Let go of those wrongs they've done to you. Get that bitterness out of your life. That's the only way you're going to truly be free. You will be amazed at what can happen in your life when you release all that poison."

—Joel Osteen

Today, I can honestly say that I am healed, I am whole, and I am ready for love and abundance. I no longer use this traumatic life occurrence as a crutch but more so as a tool to share my story and to empower other women who have experienced a degree of childhood trauma and negative life experiences that have hindered them from being the best version of themselves. I now own and operate a successful corporation that allows me to speak on global platforms to women about the power of forgiveness and walking in your divine purpose, and to mentor them privately to transform their lives from hurt to healing. I encourage women to tap into their pain and dig deep to uncover the invisible enemies that hold us hostage so that they can write their personal power stories. My biggest reward from my healing is my renewed relationship with my daughter and my ability to give and receive true love in abundance.

Everybody has a story—one that is complete with a beginning and a middle chapter. It's up to you how you write your ending. Most times, we tell our story in draft format—the incomplete, redlined version of the story that we know will be changed and edited each time we take a closer step toward finding our best self. The downside to that is, when we tell the story in draft, we are continuously reliving the hurt, the pain, the betrayal, the abuse, the mental anguish, and the suffering that we felt since the beginning of the chapter. Give yourself permission to write your ending—your way—without judgment and ridicule from others. Give yourself permission to be free from the hurt through your acts of forgiveness. Allow yourself to close out the chapter victoriously so that you can tell your story with conviction and for the sole purpose of helping another person heal.

> *"If you are not the hero of your own story, then you are missing the whole point of your humanity."*
>
> —Steve Maraboli

To be continued …

Who Am I?

Written by
Ida Robinson

Ida Robinson

Who am I? A corporate career woman, founder of Inspiring Young Moms with a Vision, and blogger of momnpowerment.com. Some would say I am doing pretty well for myself. The reality is, I am a two-time teen mom whose experiences growing up were not perfect. When I was young, my family moved from shelter to shelter until my mom was placed in a permanent low-income public housing project in Washington, D.C. Our living environment was both stable and unstable. Both of my parents lived in our home although my dad was legally not allowed, as men were not allowed to live on the premises of public housing. My parents were functioning heroin addicts. Our neighborhood was full of poverty, crime, and violence. I was an adolescent girl surrounded by dysfunction. I made a lot of bad decisions as a young lady, but I blame no one. I am a firm believer of ditching the "blame game"! And I refuse to allow my past to define me.

As I share my journey of finding myself as a young teenage parent, you will begin to understand why I have a passion for helping others survive these same adversities.

"Girls who dream become women with vision."
—Unknown

I started having sex during my first year of junior high school. I was not promiscuous, but I wasn't a virgin either. I experienced several toxic relationships at a very young age. Growing up, certain behaviors had not been defined to me adequately, so when my boyfriend showed jealousy and controlling behaviors, I assumed it was cute. I thought that he loved me because he wanted to know where I was all of the time. He got angry when I talked to other boys or smiled too hard, which led to fights, but I thought that was another way he was showing love! As I matured, I began to understand these behaviors are signs of domestic violence.

I first met the father of my son in middle school, and we did not get along. But after we got to know each other outside of school, while hanging out in the same crowds, I got to know him as a person, and we started dating in high school. And like every teen girl in my high school, I thought that being in an exclusive relationship was cool.

During my freshman year in high school, I received news that would change my life forever. I was pregnant! Although I grew up fast and had sex at a young age, I never thought I was "that girl" who would get pregnant in high school. My dreams were to attend college so I could escape poverty and set myself up for success.

I knew I was not ready to be someone's mother, but having an abortion was not an option. When I told my mom, she was supportive and scheduled my first doctor's appointment. However, when I told my dad, the reaction was much different. It was clear that his feelings were hurt. He wanted so much more for me.

His reaction shocked me but changed my perspective to my entire situation. I then felt I had something to prove. My determination to succeed was beyond my imagination, despite my pregnancy.

Growing up in the projects, it was not rare to see a young girl walking the streets with a protruding belly; so in my neighborhood, I fit right in. However, the reactions of those around me (in school, doctor's offices, and public places) made the thought of becoming a teen mother a harder pill to swallow. I went to the doctor to confirm my pregnancy, and when I entered the building, it was clear that I was not the only pregnant teen mom in the sitting area. My doctor was an older African American guy who, in my eyes, had a personal vendetta against pregnant teens. He never made my visits pleasant. He always made smart and sarcastic comments that I was too uncomfortable to address. He constantly talked negatively about teen pregnancy and expressed his views of the many statistics surrounding the issue. In my opinion, his actions were unethical. His behavior taught me that when a teenager gets pregnant, society often gives up on them altogether.

As time went by, my teachers began to recognize my protruding bulge and started asking questions: What are your plans for your future? How are you going to take care of a child? Although many teens in my school were either pregnant or already parents, something about my situation seemed different. At least that is what I thought. I continued to go to school and prepare myself for my unborn child. I was excited, but I suffered with the thought that I was delaying my dreams.

Despite the challenges and obstacles you will face, continue to reach within for greatness and unleash your best self. Don't allow others or self-sabotage to stop you from dreaming.

Lying in the bed with the urge to use the bathroom, I moved rapidly to release the urine that was screaming to get out, not realizing my water was breaking. I jumped up with urgency and, still pulling my pants up, screamed down the hall for my mom: "Mom, the baby is coming!"

My mom panicked a little more than I did. Although she was a functioning heroin addict, she was on point when it came to her children. She started asking question after question. "Are you in pain? How far apart are your contractions? Do you see any blood?" On and on and on.

We finally arrived at the hospital. Everything was moving in slow motion. I could not believe I was about to be someone's mother. I struggled with emotions of joy and resentment. The nurses checked me in at the front desk and rolled me to my room in a wheelchair. After hours of labor, I finally gave birth to my beautiful bundle of joy. My baby boy weighed seven pounds, six ounces, and was twenty-one inches long.

As a new mom, I felt a greater sense of urgency to succeed. Giving birth to my son made me look at life in a different light. It was imperative to provide for him and give him the stability I never had. Him growing up in shelters and being raised in the projects was not an option. My life had to change drastically, and I was the only person who could make that happen. Newfound determination was born in me through my son.

After three weeks of maternity rest, I went back to school. My teachers were very concerned, as the majority of them knew I had recently had a C-section. My teacher warned me daily of the dangers of hemorrhaging from climbing several flights of stairs. At that time, everything they told me went in one ear and out of the other. I stayed focused on finishing school and creating a better future for my child. I was very thankful for my mother and my son's paternal grandmother for supporting me while I continued my education.

My child went on my mom's welfare check, which meant she received an additional $100 per month from the state. Because I was only sixteen, I could not apply for public assistance. For the most part, she gave me what belonged to the baby each month, but some months, she dabbled in my money. I did not complain much because she was very supportive when it came to taking care of him.

Meanwhile, I was a teen mom preparing to graduate from high school and found myself pregnant again.

Artificial Beauté

When I graduated in June 1998, I was three months pregnant with my second child, whose father was not the same man as my first child. I started to wonder, am I falling right into the category of many teen moms? The same ones I vowed not to duplicate? Were those statistics right?

Remember, you can overcome the stereotypes associated with teen parenting. Do not allow your environment or your peers to dictate your future. Keep pushing on.

Eager to do better, I enrolled in New Heights, a basic computer/job readiness program offered by the city. I had to do something until I found employment. I enrolled my son into daycare and began the program.

February 9, 1999, the day I gave birth to my second child, was a reality check. I was nineteen with two kids and unemployed—this was not my dream life. I reached out to a friend and asked her to put a good word in for me at her job. I was excited when she told me that I had an interview scheduled, and the interview was a breeze. Things were starting to look better. Working on a federal government contract, getting paid $10.60 per hour, I was ecstatic! Things were looking up—or so I thought.

Three months later, I moved into my new apartment, and so much happened right after that. My parents lost their apartment, and my sister and I were forced to take one of them. My father came with me, and my mother went with my sister. We switched it up from time to time, but for the most part, my dad stayed with me. Shortly after, my father fell very ill, going in and out of the hospital, and my mother was silently suffering from depression. My support system was slowly fading away.

A year later, at the age of twenty-one, I buried my dad. Three months later, my mom suffered a seizure and a stroke caused by her depression, so she was placed in a nursing home. Heartbroken, but hungrier to succeed, I knew the only way I'd ever be able to provide for my children independently would be to go to college and get my degree. My initial plans were to work part-time and go to school full-time. I thought my second son's father could pick up where my parents left off. My oldest son was in grade school, and my youngest stayed home with his dad and me.

As a full-time employee, I went to my supervisor and asked if I could change my schedule to part-time so I could attend school. I didn't think this would be a problem because we already had an employee working this shift and attending school. But my request was denied. Very disappointed, I went home and thought carefully about my next move. I decided to resign from my job to attend school, figuring that I had a plan. My younger son's father stayed home with our son, and he would watch my oldest son from when he got home from school until I got home.

This schedule worked for a while until things started to get out of control. I would come home to a house that looked like pigs played in it all day. It seemed like my son's father would sleep all day and let the kids run wild. One day, I came home to the blinds from the boy's room on the floor in the living room, eggs cracked on the floors as if the kids had had an egg fight. On top of that, because my son's father was in the house all day, the moment I walked in, he walked out. Saying I missed my parents was an understatement.

Needless to say, we continued this routine until my first semester was over. Solely depending on my son's father for everything made me rethink my decision. I decided it was time to go back to work. My first thought was to begin applying for jobs, but something told me to contact my previous supervisor. Putting my pride to the side, I called my old supervisor and said, "Ms. Carry, I am ready to come back to work." Not knowing what to expect, I received a call the next day from human resources with my start date. This taught me two things: I must have been a great employee, and I would have to attend school part-time while working full-time until my finances were stable.

Making tough decisions will become your norm. You are no longer only responsible for you. Face the fight, ask hard questions, and make responsible decisions.

Ida Robinson

The Split

In 2001, after being together for three years, my youngest son's father and I separated, and I made the hard choice of allowing my youngest son to live with his dad as I continued my education. I relocated near my sister for moral support. I moved into an income subsidy apartment, which no longer went according to my income. I had a lot of financial responsibilities as a single parent: market rent, utilities, and a car note. I enrolled my oldest son in elementary school with my nephews so he could walk to and from school with them, and because my sister and I lived down the street from one another, I was able to go directly to school after work because my son stayed at her house until I returned home. With the support of my sister, I assumed working full-time and attending school would be a breeze, but I didn't realize at the time that I was so busy focusing on our future that I didn't have much time to focus on my children.

Phone calls started pouring in every day about my oldest son's behavior in class. It got to the point that every time my son's teacher's number popped up on the caller ID, my tears would start to flow. I thought I was doing everything right and figured I was a good parent. My child didn't want for anything materialistic: he had a roof over his head, clothes on his back, and food on the table. I thought I was the best mom. I was working, going to school, and trying not to be a statistic, but overall, I was failing my sons.

I didn't worry too much about my youngest child because he was living with his paternal grandmother and his father, so he was getting the attention he deserved, but I was failing my oldest son, the one who depended solely on me. His father had died in a car accident when he was six, and he needed me more than I even realized.

I began to notice that my obsession with success was not in the best interest of my child and by believing what I was doing was best for my kids, I was being the definition of selfish. With my parents no longer there to pick up my slack, I had to make some hard decisions. I chose to withdraw from my classes, move to a better neighborhood, and transfer my son. Being a supportive and attentive parent was my new role. My degree could wait. Being a federal government employee at age twenty-four was going to have to be enough at that time.

I had to make some changes. I had to be a parent, not just a provider. I had to understand that my success would come and that my children were my responsibility. I had to understand that money is not everything, and time is valuable to a child's well-being. I had to accept the fact that my parents were not there. I had to put my kids first! I thank God for my youngest son's father's family, as they provided support during a time in my life when I was trying not only to figure the parenting thing out but trying to survive and learn adulthood all alone.

My biggest takeaway was learning to shift when necessary and not be complacent about my situation. I experienced many adversities that required me to make tough choices. Although all of my choices were not the best, I learned from them and moved forward. I taught myself to be strong and regained my parenthood identity before it was too late. Raising males in this society is already hard, but as a single teen mom, you realize this through trial and error.

Because I learned from my mistakes and had the ability to make tough choices and strategically plan out my next move in life (for my children and me), I was able to go from sixteen and pregnant to thirty-six and six figures. As a federal government employee, I worked intentionally to receive multiple promotions throughout my career. My sons both graduated high school and grew into successful young men. I also have an eleven-year-old daughter who is making straight As and Bs in school, and I am a proud grandmother of two.

I am blessed and highly favored. Only by the Grace of God was I able to survive my story. I want to thank my daughter's father for stepping up to the plate with my boys in their dads' absences (both of my sons lost their biological father at a very young age). Now, I am working diligently to inspire other young moms to live their dreams unselfishly. Despite the circumstances, with action, dreams come true.

Artificial Beauté

You have the ability to write your vision. Your past does not define you. Statistics do not define you.

What I learned through my obstacles of being a teen mom:

- You can still be successful after giving birth; however, remember the moment you have a child that your child should be your priority.
- Utilize government resources as stepping stones to your independence, but never become dependent on government assistance.
- Accept support but don't lose your parenthood identity.
- Use contraception to avoid unplanned pregnancy.
- Open communication is key to effective parenting.
- Life still happens after you become a parent. Learn to cope with adversity, and make tough decisions for the benefit of your family.
- Be comfortable with shifting. Change is good.

Breaking Down the Scaffold

The Battle Is Over – The Journey Begins

Written by
Anne Sewell

Anne Sewell

She is clothed with strength and dignity, and she laughs without fear of the future."
—Proverbs 31:25 NLT

This was the happiest day of my life. I had received my transcript from the guidance counselor and confirmed I would be graduating from high school in June with honors. I was happy, full of joy and hope for my future. It seemed like I had waited years for this transformation into adulthood. I was a young woman, full of self-confidence, seeking a life of happiness, love, success, and abundance. I was celebrating life—after all, it was my eighteenth birthday, a very special day, and there I was, standing in front of my school that soon would be my alma mater.

Yes indeed, my visions were awesome. My mind, body, and soul were dedicated to my dreams, and all my hard work would soon be rewarded. I had made it. I stood there visualizing the next steps in my life, my adrenaline running wild. I knew I would succeed in my dreams and visions and become a successful entrepreneur. I was an honor roll student, in the pep club, a majorette, a cheerleader, and I was voted Most Likely to Succeed. I had been recruited to attend Eastern Airline Flight Attendant School in Florida. Of course, this was back in the seventies, and that was an accomplishment. You had to have a petite frame, long hair, a radiant complexion, and outstanding customer care skills. I met all the requirements; plus, I had the biggest drive to succeed. I was committed to becoming a successful woman, and I was ready to fulfill the requirements of hard work, dedication, determination, and discipline.

Stay focused in your visions, dreams, and creativity. They are your gifts from God.

I was young, talented, intelligent, and attractive, but I was very naive in many ways. I knew very little about relationships. I lived a sheltered life. My parents were like the gravy on mashed potatoes, or ketchup on fries—they watched every move I made. They were so protective that, secretly, I called them "the wardens." Being that I was the only girl of five children, my parents left no doors unlocked. It felt like I lived inside a bubble, and there were so many things I wasn't allowed to do. Unlike my girlfriends, I didn't date, go to parties, hang out on the step, go to the mall, or wear lipstick, stockings, or designer anything. I had plenty, as my parents would say, along with a curfew of 6:00 p.m. on weekdays.

Suddenly, a loud noise brought me back to reality. My girlfriends were singing out loud and calling my name: "Girl, he's finer than wine, and he wants to meet you." I started walking closer, swinging my long ponytail, bangs laying over my left eye. There he was,

Mr. MVA—so fine, tall, and slim, and smelling so good. He was dressed to kill and, little did I know, he would almost do just that to me. He was driving a brand new, fully equipped convertible vehicle with leather seats, a design in the back window, and white wall tires. He represented money! Yes, that was my number one goal in life: to have plenty of money by any means necessary.

"For the love of money is the root of all evil."
--1 Timothy 6:10 KJV

There we were making eye contact. The chemistry between us showed the connection of true love and togetherness in every way possible. Is this what love at first sight feels like? I thought to myself. I claimed it, I wanted it, and yes, it felt good.

He said to me, "You are a fine young lady, and I want to make you mine."

Explore the word "mine," used as possession, control, and ownership.

I was blushing like the inexperienced teenager I was. Of course, he did not know I was as young as I was (I found out later that he was eight years older). I accepted the compliments and gave it all back to him. We exchanged numbers, he kissed my hand, and *wow*, I exploded. He was the kind of guy I dreamt about, and he was seeking my heart. Little did he know, he already had it, and little did I know, he would destroy me mentally and physically at the same damn time.

Once I got home, my girlfriends burned up my phone to get the 411: What's his name? How old is he? He got any brothers or friends? Do he have a job? One thing we all forgot to ask was if he was married. In that moment, I realized the only thing I knew about him was his name: Mr. MVA. Of course, I wasn't even sure of that. I just knew he was fine. Naturally, I needed to get more information about this mystery man if we were to have any chance at a future. So when he called, I would get all the info I needed.

As I waited for his call, it began to get late. I had no homework and did not have to work, and I was overwhelmed with all the excitement, so I decided to start dinner. When my mom got home, we could talk, and I would fill her in on my new adventure of my male companion. Did I say that? I had already made him mine without knowing anything but his name, which I knew wasn't his real name, but it would do for now.

Then, there it was—the phone rang. I ran to answer it, my heart skipping beats. I was not sure if it was healthy, but it sure felt good. It was him.

"Hello, may I please speak with my heartbeat?"

"Who?" I asked, at first pretending I didn't know who he was. Then, giving in, I said, "This is she."

"Hello my heartbeat."

I said, "Hello." If he only knew my heart was beating like a generator pumping electricity. He was calling to make sure I made it home safely and if we could do lunch the next day. I did not hesitate to say yes but was hoping I didn't sound too anxious. He said that he would pick me up at noon, setting the time before checking to see if I was available.

Never let anyone make plans with or for you without checking your availability; this is a sign of control.

He said good night, and before I could ask him any questions or have a conversation, he hung up.

Take time to communicate and be a part of the conversation; don't let the other party take control. After all, it takes two to communicate.

The morning came so fast, and the sun was shining so beautifully in my room. I jumped up from my bed and saw it was 9:30 a.m. What day was it? Had I overslept? Oh my goodness—it was Saturday, and my lunch date was at noon with Mr. MVA. I realized that he didn't know where I lived. Let me call him now and give him my address, I thought. I dialed his number, and the recording said the number was not in service. I assumed

Artificial Beauté

I had dialed an incorrect number, so I tried again, and the recording said the same: the number you are calling is not in service. Well I'll be damned. Fine as wine, smelling so good, and lying through the gap in his teeth.

Ladies, don't admire the book cover; you better start reading its contents.

It was time to get ready for my date, and I was thinking of ways to approach Mr. MVA about his number and some other things I wanted to know. But I first needed to ask my mom if it was okay. Yes, at eighteen, I was still asking for approval. I wasn't sure of his age, where he lived, if he was married, or if he had a job—these were the questions my mom was going to ask me, and I didn't have a clue. I wasn't sure if I wanted to tell her about the mystery man. I decided to wait to tell her the truth and instead tell her I was going out with the girls. She would say, "Be home before midnight," like she always did when my girlfriends and I got together on the weekends.

I was wearing my finest dress, smelling good with all the accessories. Yes, I was aiming to impress my date. My first date. I was so excited and feeling mature.

My mom looked at me with approval and said, "This must be a special hangout with the girls."

I immediately froze and realized this was the first

time I was going to tell my mother a lie. This was not starting out well. "Yes, Mom, we are having a senior graduate celebration party." Wow, I thought of that quick.

She gave me a hug and one of her mommy's baby kisses and said, "I am so proud of you."

One lie leads to another.

On the outside, my body felt good, but on the inside, I was burning with deceit. He would be picking me up soon, and if my mom saw him and his car, she would not only ground me for lying, but she would embarrass me. I would never survive this. Lord, help me—here comes my religious background—two lies within ten minutes. My thirteen faces were beginning to come to play. I called out to my mom that I was leaving and would be home by midnight. She told me to have a good time, to be safe, and that she loved me. I left feeling the weight of the world on me. I started walking to the corner, which was on the same street but out of sight of my house, so I could wait for him. God, forgive me, I prayed, hoping no one would see me while I waited for my date. The wait seemed like it was forever, but then he appeared. He stepped out of the car, took me by the hand, and held my face in his hands.

He said to me, "I have been waiting for you all my

life," and kissed me with one of the most passionate kisses I will ever experience.

Well, that was the beginning, I thought. This will be my love for life. He opened the door for me, and I got in the car. He was truly a gentleman after my heart.

"So where would you like to go?"

That was the million-dollar question. Hell, I didn't know; anywhere but McDonald's or Roy Rogers.

I immediately went into my intellectual mode and said, "I would love to go and do anything you suggest." Intellectual? More like dumb. I think I just set myself up for the play. This man, pretty boy or whoever, could be a rapist, serial killer, hustler, pimp, or whatever. My goodness, I told no one where I was going or who I was with. I didn't even know where he was taking me.

We started our journey to where he was taking me for lunch, and as we approached the venue, it was something out of a fairy tale: a beautiful oceanfront restaurant with an amazing view from the top.

"So, baby, is this okay? I just want to do any and everything in this world to make you happy. You are my one and only heartbeat. I love you, baby." He placed another one of them kisses on me, and I was done. *Take me, I'm yours, forever.*

The lunch was magnificent, and the walk on the beach under the sunset was breathtaking. We played and wrote our names in the sand and circled it with hearts. I felt so good and safe with him. We talked about so many things, but he still asked me to call him

MVA. Of course I was curious about what it stood for, and he told me that, in time, I would understand.

He eventually asked me if I was ready to go home. I wanted to spend the rest of that night and my life with him, but it was getting late, and I had a curfew. We made a pact that he would pick me up every day after school and take me to and from work. I could live with that.

"Good night, baby. Remember, my heart only beats for you, and I love you."

"I love you too." Did I say that? Oh well, it felt good.

After only a month into the relationship, a lot had transpired that gave me the signal to get out. Mr. MVA had a lot going on, and I didn't understand or relate to some of the things he did, but he said it was all for me.

He invited me to the Annual Players Ball. He bought me one of the most expensive, elegant gowns that I have owned to this day. There I was, dressed in red, accessories to match, and flawless hair with my bang over my eye, not realizing at the time that my bang would become a permanent shield so you could not see the blackness and puffiness from his hits and slaps.

I was praying for the night to be unforgettable and it was. We danced to the music, and he held me so close. I felt safe and secure in his arms. But that feeling would soon come to an end and have me in a very dark place in my life. To place a cap on the night, I lost a part of my life that could never be restored—my virginity. I was raped by the man who said he was in love with me.

My "no" meant nothing to him. Fear, control, denial, and self-destruction took control.

I felt so alone and taken aback by the drama, I started to build my scaffold for protection. I cried out to God, "Why is this happening to me? My God, why me?" I prayed daily. "I believe in God, I love God, and I go to church. Why is this happening to me?" I was so afraid of this man and yet I loved him so much—or so I thought.

I was somewhat still in my right mind the next day, but fear had taken supremacy over me. I had been raped. My God, I meant nothing to him. He had stolen my first time with force, fear, and so much pain, and it still resides in my mental memory. He was not the same person from our first date, and I knew I had to get away from the relationship immediately and never see this man again. I had not spoken to him for several days, and I thought he would realize what he had done and apologize. I was not going to accept it and planned on letting him know I was moving on.

Then the day came when I experienced the second episode of control and abuse in front of my school, where I was to graduate in a few months. I had not talked to or seen him in a week and was feeling a breath of relief that I could move forward, even though he had stolen the precious moments of giving myself with tenderness and true love to that special one.

I was still in a daze and decided to walk across the street to Soul Burger, where all the students hung out. I bought a double cheeseburger and fries to go. Everyone was asking where the convertible ride was—they hadn't seen it lately. Suddenly, he appeared from out of nowhere, and yes, my heart skipped many beats—but it wasn't from loving him. I was terrified of him and what he was about to do. *My God, help me.* What must I do: Walk away? Or stand up and let him know it was over.

My future flashed in front of my eyes: soon I would be leaving to go to school, and all this would be behind me. I told him I didn't want to see him anymore; he had hurt me, took my virginity, disrespected me, and it was over. I was explaining to him this was not the way love should be, and suddenly, Mr. MVA hit me so hard with his fist. That's the only thing I can remember: the cheeseburger going up in the air, disappearing, never returning. Blood poured from my eye and nose. The pain and swelling was unbearable.

If they hit you once, they will hit you again, again, and again. Get out. Walk away.

To this day, I will not eat a cheeseburger because of what it represents to me. The hit was so hard and painful. I then surrendered my all to him. He had captured all my insecurities, made me powerless, and controlled my life for the next twenty years. The mental and physical abuse was so excruciating; the fear and the control became my addictions. I continued to build my scaffold for protection from my abuser, thinking it would protect me temporarily until I figured a way to escape. My walls grew thicker and thicker and became an inner mass of fear, pain, and failure. The gift of life lay trapped within the walls of captivity by my abuser.

My relationship with my abuser was years of living hell. He was so generous with materialistic giving that I became confused about what a life of happiness was. I wanted to walk away so many times, but the fear and threats of killing me and my family lay in my mind and heart. The physical and mental attacks from my abuser became part of my daily living. I began believing that was the way life should be. I was lost and trapped in a dark place, and I didn't want anyone to know what I was going through, so there I stayed in my walls of protection. I knew I had to find a way to escape from allowing the evil force to take supremacy over my life with artificial love, money, and false pretenses. He took control of my mind, body, and soul, which didn't belong to him.

If you love yourself, and the gift of life God gave you, surrender your all and stay in faith and keep your mind open to his word.

I lived in a very abusive life with my ex. He had serious

issues, and I can see them now. I truly had a hard time sharing these small hidden abusive attacks, and there is so much more. Each time I write, I still cry, but they are tears of joy. I pray daily for any woman in an abusive relationship to seek help; it's a deadly experience. What hurts even more is the mental breakdown on you. You forgive but you never forget.

Yes, there were trials and tribulations in my life, and times when I felt I was alone. I went back to my daily worship, praise, and prayer, but my night became shorter when the voice of the Almighty spoke to me and said, "My child, he's only able to do to you what you allow. I am your protector and provider. Walk with me in the name of the Holy Spirit." God was there with me through the twenty years of hell, and when I surrendered my life back to Him and asked for His forgiveness for placing another above Him, my life began to change for the good.

Worship and praise your heavenly father and not those of the flesh. Abuse is an illness, and to allow yourself to be abused is an addiction.

I fear no other than my Lord and Savior (Psalm 19:9), and I pray daily: "Father God, I choose to obey You. You said that we are to forgive others. I choose to forgive everyone who has ever hurt me. I release them, if there is any hurt in my heart from them. God, my heart is hurting and broken, and I open it up for you to heal me, because I have forgiven." It isn't a feeling; it's called obedience.

I am now walking in faith and extending an invitation to all to witness the spiritual transformation of my life and watch me break down the scaffold. I am now a woman of defining characteristics, sustainable possibilities, and gravitating abundance. I am fearfully and wonderfully made, and there are no limitations on who or what I can be. I was born with tendencies, good and bad. My choices, fear, and lack of knowledge placed me in the dark and damp places. I allowed the fear of human flesh to hold me in bondage. I became so angry, full of hate, heartless, and suicidal and had the strong desire to kill the evil flesh. Life meant nothing to me. Now, I walk out in FAITH: Forever Able in the Holy Spirit. I know through my spiritual faith, forgiveness, and obedience that I can conquer all things. The battle was not mine to fight and I was not alone. I had to surrender my all to God and let the spirit lead me through. I am free!

"The Lord is my light and my salvation; whom shall I fear? The Lord is the strength of my life; Of whom shall I be afraid?"

—Psalm 27:1 KJV

Who's Cheating Who?

All the Time, I Was Cheating Myself

Written by
LuDrean Peterson

LuDrean Peterson

"And forgive us our debts, as we forgive our debtors."
—Matthew 6:12 KJV

At a very young age, my mother taught my sister and me "The Lord's Prayer." We were praised by church members for our ability to fully recite Matthew 6:9-13. We memorized the popular verses that begin with verse 9, "Our Father," and end with verse 13, "Amen." You will soon learn that it took me more than thirty years later to learn that this verse wasn't the end of my story.

Forgiveness has been one of the most challenging topics and actions that I have dealt with in my life. In the past, I focused heavily on trying to make the other person pay for their wrongdoings. I felt like forgiving someone meant that I was cheated. I felt like it would mean that I was giving up my rights to demand respect from that person. I felt as if I would be allowing someone to take something from me.

Refusing to forgive became habitual, and my low tolerance for wrongdoing became my defense mechanism. Thus, my verbal abuse toward anyone who came my way was severe. I know I intimidated people with my words and looks. But again, that was my defense mechanism. If someone did me wrong, I was going to teach them a lesson. People would often say that my slick tongue was sharper than a two-edged sword. My staredowns and stern looks would cause people to think twice before coming at me wrong. I would say hurtful things that I really didn't mean, but the goal was to protect myself. I didn't understand that I was tearing people down.

My first taste of struggling to forgive involved my relationship with my father. My sister and I would spend a great portion of our summers in South Carolina. I would head to the "block," a strip of stores on Main Street, where my father's barbershop and pool hall were located. He would place me in his barber's chair and spin me around. He would then put his face next to mine, focus my face to look in the mirror, and tell me how beautiful I was. He would give me money, and some for my sister, and I would be on my merry little way. I would frequent the barbershop throughout my stay and then wouldn't really have much contact with him until the following summer. The challenges of an absentee father can impact children in various ways, some negative and some positive. For many years, all I could see from my lens were the negative sides.

The positive thoughts and memories that I had of my father died in the summer of 1983. That was the year that I got "too grown" for my South Carolina summer visits. That is when I began building my wall, developing my defense mechanisms, and closely guarding my circle. I was extremely selective about who I allowed in my space. I was able to handle the absence of my father for periods of time, but it never failed that something would pop up in my life that would make me think of him.

The family tree homework assignment in school was the worst. I would write my father's name in but would leave the remaining side of the tree blank. I wouldn't share my family tree homework assignment with my mom. I didn't want to ask for her help with my paternal side because I assumed that she would have felt like I didn't appreciate her. While she never bad-mouthed my father, she didn't appear too happy when I praised whatever I got from him. My mother would remind me that she worked very hard during the day and then came home to cook and care for us on a daily basis. I felt that she was non-verbally implying that what my father did wasn't worthy of my celebrations. I better understood her unspoken words as I grew older.

I was cautious of allowing people in my space, and I focused on self because of my refusal to allow anyone the opportunity to abandon, disappoint, or hurt me like my father had. My attitude was to not accept anything that I didn't like from anyone.

In elementary school, my interests were making friends and having fun. When I started junior high, around the same time I stopped going to South Carolina, I felt like a new chapter of my life had begun. I went to school with a "no friends needed," "focus on your schoolwork" attitude. I was determined to excel in my academics and stay out of trouble so that I could be successful. Growing up, I felt that the more successful I was, the more regret my father would have because he would not be counted as a contributor to making it happen. I wanted him to feel like I was better off without him and that he was missing out by not being in my life.

Eventually, I went from "no friends" to having a small circle of friends. During the first week of school, I met two friends and developed special relationships from our first encounters, and I gained a number of friends throughout junior high school; however, I still kept my stance that if you wronged me, it was over.

I went to an out-of-boundary high school, H.D. Woodson. There, I met my best friend, and we had the greatest times of our lives. We really vibed and understood one another. After several years, later into our mid-twenties, we fell out over something that, in hindsight, is so small. She had just gotten a new home telephone number that not that many people knew. A former male friend called her home, and her boyfriend at the time convinced her that I may have given her old boyfriend her number. When my friend asked if I had given him her number, my exact words were, "You know me better than that. I can't believe that you just asked me that," and I hung up the phone.

I felt that my trust was being challenged. When she called back and asked for forgiveness, I wouldn't accept it. Instead, in return, I kept explaining how she should have approached the issue and what I would have done if the shoe had been on the other foot. Determined that she should pay for questioning my loyalty and for letting someone else convince her that I would have any role in hurting her, I felt that it was fair to let her hurt. Not forever—just until I was ready. But things were never the same again.

When I was finally ready to forgive her, she was ill. Being around sick people has always made me physically and emotionally nauseous, and I couldn't get myself together to see her in the hospital. She passed away, and it devastated me. I was sick for about a month. I had some words for God because I felt like He could have allowed me to bring closure to the issue. It took me almost eight years to finally be able to go to her gravesite and have that "I accept your forgiveness, please forgive me" conversation. I had cheated myself, and I ended up paying for it because I wouldn't allow anyone to become too close to me.

God forgives you based on how you forgive others. Don't cheat yourself out of God's blessing!

From the time my summer stints in South Carolina ended in 1983 to my adulthood, visits to South Carolina were infrequent and only for specific occasions such as funerals and family reunions. During these visits, I would not stop by to visit my father. He would reach out frequently to my mother to contact me, but I wasn't interested. I would send messages back to him that "children need their parents when they are younger, and I'm grown." I was determined to make him pay. But in the end, I was the one who paid. I paid by creating a wall and preventing myself from fully living and loving. I didn't trust people to do the right thing with my heart and friendship, so I held it close.

Unaddressed forgiveness caused me to hold on to unresolved hurt, and those issues spilled over into other relationships throughout my life. It impacted my role as a mother: I was overly loving and protective. It impacted my role as a wife: I remained in a relationship much longer than I should have to keep my immediate family together. I was determined that no child of mine would be subjected to grow up without their father living in their household.

My perspective began to change after a conversation with my brother, who I met via Facebook, while on a business trip in South Africa. I couldn't sleep, so I logged on to Facebook and stumbled upon a message that he had written to me months prior. I began having a dialogue with him, and he updated me on my father's health. While my brother and I were communicating, my father called him and asked him to give me his number to call if I ever wanted to reach him. As the conversation continued, my brother began to tell me the pros and cons of living in the household with our father. All of those years, I had created a story in my mind of what I had missed out on, but the stories from my brother often left me thinking and silently hearing him say, "You were probably better off with him not being in your life."

I honestly don't recall whether or not my brother actually stated it or if I summed it up from hearing how he was impacted by our father being present.

I convinced myself that 2016 was the year to truly forgive everyone who I felt had wronged me in the past or had any unresolved feelings toward. Every first week in January, I plan my leave for the entire year. That year, I had gotten to the point where I was ready to have a discussion with the goal of forgiving my father. I decided August 25 was the date. I booked the room for my trip to Myrtle Beach and to visit my father. I made the decision that this was a drive that I would need to take alone, a long road trip to help me gather my thoughts and clear my head on the return.

On August 4 at 7:53 p.m., I received a message that my father had passed away an hour before. I felt a wave of emotion that traveled from the crown of my head to the soles of my feet. After years of me choosing not to forgive and making what I felt was a huge step to forgive, I had finally mustered up the courage to go forward with this "process," and just days away from it happening, this message meant that it was now impossible. It is hard to put into words how I felt. I wanted to blame him, yet again—as if he had a say in God's timing for his life.

The question I played in my head was, "Why was he not more involved in my life?" but in a not-so-nice tone. Yet a part of me was a bit relieved from not having to have that conversation. I wanted to know, but

I wanted the answer to not hurt me, and it needed to make sense to me. Once I realized that this was a lot to ask, I wasn't sure if I was ready to hear whatever was going to be said.

For a slight moment, I thought about not attending the funeral—again, feeling like I didn't owe him, but he owed me. During my prayers, clear as day, God revealed to me that I was paid in abundance of what I deserved. I allow my friends to use my timeshare, and just weeks before, I had been checking availability in Myrtle Beach during the weekend of August 12 for a friend. This was normally one of the most challenging resorts to book during the summer months, but guess what? God. I found a room and also received an upgrade to a two-bedroom oceanfront high floor suite. So that night, I packed my bags and sent my leave request to my supervisor. The next morning, I headed to South Carolina.

"Forgive others, not because they deserve forgiveness, but because you deserve peace"

—Jonathan Lockwood Huie

Don't cheat yourself out of peace!

The wake was scheduled for the next day, Friday. The family viewing was scheduled for noon and then would open to others at 1:00 p.m. My plan was to slide in and out once it was opened to others, however, siblings were inboxing me one after another. When I got there, it was awkward except with the two siblings I had been in contact with. I didn't remember anyone else. When asked if I needed a moment alone with the body, I declined. My feelings were neutral, and I was in observation mode. His side of the family appeared to be nice and close-knit. I procrastinated on attending the family dinner, and when I decided to stop through, it had already ended.

The day of the funeral, my feelings were in the mode of *come on, let's get this over with*. I arrived five minutes late, and the family had already walked in. The preacher was preaching, so the doors of the sanctuary had been closed. I went into the ladies room to gather myself. The church was really large, and the walk to my seat felt like the longest walk ever, seeming as if I had to walk past a hundred pews to get to the front.

The next moments were very emotional. Many people went up to the podium and gave their remarks. They described my father as a direct, stubborn, and selfish person who had shifted to become a person with a great concern for others. They talked about his faith in God and dedication to church. They talked about his sheer honesty that some couldn't handle. They talked about his entrepreneurial spirit and the donations he had given to youth activities. They talked about a shift in his life where he had changed and began to show his softer side. Tears profusely and uncontrollably rolled down my face. The eulogy and some of the comments that were said about my father had been the exact words that I and others had used to describe my personal shift.

My brother, sitting to my right, held me so tight and said, "He wanted you to know that he changed his life."

My sister was to the left of me and kept handing me tissues as needed. I was overwhelmed with emotion. *Lord, where did all of these feelings come from?* I wore makeup because I did not expect to cry. All of a sudden, I missed my father and wanted to have at least that one last conversation with him. The ride to the burial site was the longest ride ever. I'm talking highways, byways, and country dirt roads. Riding in the car alone gave me time to pull myself together.

My father was buried next to his mother, my grandmother. The tears started again because I felt like this filled in a part of that empty side of the family tree homework from my childhood days. (By the way, I finally completed that family tree.) The funeral home directed a dedication to the family, and I received the memorial candle, with a picture and prayers. The tears built up again.

With the releasing of the doves, my bitterness lifted and was replaced with a feeling of peace. As the dove flew away, so did my resentment and my unwillingness to forgive, but more so, I freed myself and just allowed things to be. I picked real flowers from the arrangements, and those flowers sat on my breakfast bar for six months. Looking at them every day helped me on my forgiveness journey.

Now, I can truly say that I have forgiven my father and have asked God to forgive me for not forgiving him sooner. I realized that during the times when I was unhappy about my biological father not being there, my heavenly father was with me all along.

Throughout my journey to forgiveness, I would discuss my shift and situations with friends and share prayers asking God for help with my feeling slighted as I practiced forgiving others. There were situations when people would test me, and I would choose to walk away to avoid saying things just to hurt their feelings and to avoid saying anything that I really didn't mean. During one of my conversations with God, it hit me: God was not putting me in a position to look like a "pushover"; He was showing me a sign of my maturity. Never would I have imagined the day when someone would be able to say something inappropriate to me and get away without consequences. Through maturity, I realized that what others say really and truly does not matter. At the point of maturity, my goal changed from tearing people down to building people up!

Some time later, I learned that feeling the need to address every situation where I felt wronged or disrespected was cheating me. Responding back and forth to negative comments only drained me and often led me to saying hurtful things to others. By doing so, I was cheating myself out of a happy, worry-free, and peaceful life.

I attended a Fatherless Freedom Event and joined

a Facebook group, Healing, Transformation & Collaboration, for support on my path of forgiveness. The leader asked members to post what it felt like to be forgiven and to complete the statement, "On the other side of forgiveness…" She compiled our responses into one post; many expressed feeling "elated, mature, gratitude, relief, joy, free, humbled, cherished. and loved."

My contribution was maturity. I felt a sense of maturity to stand up and address instead of withhold problems that were causing such feelings. It is a great sentiment, and I've seen it pour into all areas of my life. I gained the lesson of knowing that not forgiving was really holding me in bondage. When you don't forgive, you are hurting yourself—not the ones who hurt you. Once I released an unforgiving hold, burdens were lifted and I felt a sense of peace.

Recall my earlier mentioning of Matthew 6: 9-13. Fast forward thirty years, and here lies one of the most pivotal moments of my life. During Bible study, we dissected Matthew 16:9-13 and went on to verse 14, which reads, *"For if ye forgive men their trespasses, your heavenly Father will also forgive you."* I learned this as a child and understood it, but it was much more impactful this time around. And then verse 15: *"But if you forgive not men their trespass, neither will your Father forgive your trespasses."* This was huge! I couldn't recall ever reading this verse. With a much deeper understanding of the meaning, I had no other choice than to rid my spirit of not forgiving people who had wronged me.

My forgiveness journey has not been easy, but once I released the spirit of forgiveness, I was truly delivered. Stop cheating yourself.

> *"When you hold on to your history, you do it at the expense of your destiny"*
>
> —Bishop T.D. Jakes

Forgive and move on. Don't cheat yourself out of your destiny!

Pain Producing Purpose

Written by
Kimberly Moorer

When I was a little girl, I dreamed of my future husband. I thought about how he would love me, take care of me, and be my best friend forever. We would raise our four kids together, two boys and two girls. It was the perfect plan in my head. As I began to date, I encountered guys who lied, cheated, and were mentally abusive, but I never lost faith in having the dream family I wanted.

One day, one of my friends told me she wanted to introduce me to her uncle. I wasn't big on being hooked up, but I thought, hey, how could it hurt? We met up, she introduced us, and sparks flew from there. We spent most of our time together, and things started to move fast. I found myself engaged and married within a two-month period. Things were finally going well in my life. I found the man who I knew was about to make my dreams a reality. Then, one day, my worst fears came true.

One night, I had a dream that my husband cheated on me. The dream felt so real that I found myself crying because of the pain I felt in the dream. I told my husband about the dream, but he vowed that no such thing had happened or would happen. So I believed him, pushing the dream to the back of my mind.

Then, I received a message that changed my life forever. A woman was on the other end of the phone telling me that she and my husband were having an affair. I was devastated beyond repair. In the back of my mind, I questioned whether she was telling the truth, but because she had so many details, I knew deep in my heart that she was. I didn't want to believe it nor did I want to accept it because, if I did, my fairy tale would surely be lost forever. I was filled with anger, rage, disappointment, and regret. I experienced so many emotions at once that I was mentally and emotionally drained. I was in desperate need for someone to save me. I wanted God and needed him like never before.

Nowhere in my plans did I include my husband cheating on me before we were married a full year. I quickly realized that my fairy tale marriage and family just might not be what I had dreamt, and that changed my perspective about life and relationships. I was looking for a husband like my dad, he was looking for a wife like his mom, and neither one of us fit that mold. In my mind, I knew what I wanted from my mate and what I was willing to give, so I thought it would work out like that, not factoring in the idea that I only had control over myself and what I did or didn't do. Although I realized I hadn't in fact married a man like my dad, I accepted the choice I made and moved forward, trying to be the best wife I could be and make the best out of everything and everyone in my life.

During this time, I had trouble confiding in others about what was going on because they were all quick to say "you must forgive him" and "you made a vow to be with him through the good and the bad." To hear that angered me even more. I didn't want to hear that at all. I felt as though no one truly understood how I felt, especially if they had never experienced that betrayal themselves. I was at an all-time low and didn't know how I would ever begin to pick myself up again, trust again, or move on with life as if nothing had ever happened. After all, I'm human—not God. In my mind, I began to question what I could have done to prevent him from cheating on me. How could I have been a better wife, mate, and friend? I blamed myself!

Never judge yourself based on a decision someone else made concerning you.

As bitterness began to take root, I began to feel unwanted, unneeded, and undesired. I thought to myself, why wasn't I enough? I was trapped in my own thoughts, feeling sorry for myself. I became somewhat depressed and troubled in my spirit. Although I did not reveal how I was truly feeling in front of people, I knew that I was dying on the inside. I became mean, cold, and disconnected from my husband and anyone else who decided to tell me what I needed to do during my time of grieving and pain. In some ways, I wanted help—I needed help—but in other ways, I felt no one could truly help me get past this low point in my life. I put up walls that no one could climb over or break through. I know it is said that if you have a wall up, no one can get in or get out, but I was okay with that because I was no longer willing to give myself to anyone who was willing to hurt me.

The pain was so deep, I became numb to any and everything that looked like it would affect me. I became emotionally detached from everything. Why? Because I didn't want anyone to ever hurt me that way again or have any kind of control over my emotions but me. Trust was not even up for discussion because no one was getting it, and if you did get a little bit, it was only because you did something to earn it. In my mind, I wondered, how could I truly love again?

My husband begged for my forgiveness and another chance to make things right. But how could I love my husband the way God wanted me to love when I didn't feel that he was worthy of the love that I had once given so freely—the love that he had abused and taken advantage of? But despite how I truly felt within, I continued to go to church, go to work, and be a wife because that was my life, and I had to keep living. I refused to live as a shell.

We had some good days and some bad days. There were times when I wanted to love my husband, but I couldn't because I secretly resented him for what he did to me. Although he knew that he hurt me, I questioned whether he really understood how I truly felt. I contemplated divorce many times but thought to myself, did I really want to be by myself again? I thought about how I would feel ashamed and embarrassed about what people would think if I got divorced—what people would think of me professing to love God and being His servant but being a sinner at the same time because I decided to leave my husband for being unfaithful.

There were times when I would be in a room full of people but I would feel so alone because no one could feel the pain I was going through. I hated when the holidays came because I had to put a smile on my face and pretend to have all this love in my heart, acting like I had it all together. I felt like a hypocrite because I had all the material things that anyone could ask for or need, but the things I truly longed to have within or from my mate were so far away from me. I became so consumed with what I thought was my failure that I couldn't see past any of it to see a brighter future.

When the memory of the affair came back, I would question him like a private investigator about the details that I thought I needed to know to bring me closure. I also wondered why I would keep asking him when all he would do was lie. Our relationship declined more and more as time went on. I was tired of going through the cycles of bickering and arguing, and I realized that I could no longer continue to go down the same path. I was desperate for change and a new direction, and all I had left was to seek God for answers. I was lost in the wilderness of my own thoughts. If you would have asked me before I began to go through this battle about my faith, I would have said that I had very strong faith, but after this bout of hurt, I started to question it all.

The betrayal made me want to be rebellious too

because I felt I didn't deserve to be going through what I was going through. Of course, I wanted revenge. I was hurting and I wanted him to feel my pain, but I also had to remind myself that certain behaviors weren't a part of my character. I questioned if I was starting to abandon what I had been taught or what I knew was the right thing to do. I faced those questions and decisions for some time.

I was drowning in my own self-pity until, one day, God spoke to me! He showed me my reflection and reminded me of how much He loved me. He reminded me of what His word says in 1 Corinthians 13:4-8 KJV:

> *Charity suffereth long, and is kind; charity envieth not; charity vaunteth not itself, is not puffed up, Doth not behave itself unseemly, seeketh not her own, is not easily provoked, thinketh no evil; Rejoiceth not in iniquity, but rejoiceth in the truth; Beareth all things, believeth all things, hopeth all things, endureth all things. Charity never faileth: but whether there be prophecies, they shall fail; whether there be tongues, they shall cease; whether there be knowledge, it shall vanish away.*

Needless to say, God got me together. I repented for all the things I did and said out of anger, bitterness, and hurt. I knew I had to move forward, but I had no idea how. Somewhere in my mind, I was stuck in between my ugly past and the beautiful future I could have. I began to take one day at a time because thinking too far ahead made me nervous, but not thinking about the future at all made me a little sad because I wanted to continue to have hope and faith that things would one day be on the other side of where I currently was. Some days, because I had made the choice to stay, I thought that it meant I had forgiven him. But when he would exhibit some of the same patterns (keeping secrets, adding passcodes to electronics, not wanting to be intimate, etc.), all my negative emotions would return. That meant that all my effort and work was lost. As time went on, I felt like I was able to move forward. I was finally in a better place; we were in a good place—a place that I hadn't thought possible.

After being married for three years, the fact that we had not been able to conceive was devastating. But we continued to pray, while others prayed with us, and we became pregnant with our son within the next year. My faith began to rebuild, and I began to trust again, to love again, to honor and cherish again. Life was great. Because of that, I knew that forgiving was essential to moving forward, to having a beautiful life unbound by past hurts, betrayal, and pain. We were enjoying parenthood and a newfound love and respect for each other.

Months later, we purchased a brand new home that God blessed us with. I was on cloud nine, thanking God for this newfound faith, joy, and love he had given me. I found myself thinking, what more could I ask for? Things were heading in the right direction and, at that point, I was glad I hadn't given up. No matter what I was feeling or how hard it got, if I had given up, I wouldn't have my beautiful son.

Over six years had passed when one day, I decided to check our phone records online. It had been about three years since I'd looked at them last. I found a recurring number. There was a nervous feeling in my gut that told me that I really didn't want to know, but I had the burning desire to know. As I dialed the number and the phone rang, I was beginning to regret my decision, but it was too late to turn back. Finally, there was an answer.

"Hello." The mystery person that was only once a number now had a voice, and it was in fact a woman on the receiving end of the phone. I asked her how she knew my husband and what they had to talk about so much during the times I wasn't around. She responded saying they were friends getting to know each other and they talked to each other about their relationships. They had spent months conversing back and forth, so I knew there was more to it than that. I lost all sense of control. I was back at that place I was years ago, but this time was worse. I had a son to think about and the possibility of losing our home and starting over.

My life had, again, turned upside down in a matter of minutes. There I was, back to being angry, disappointed, confused, and unsure of what to do. I couldn't just act like it didn't matter. After I confronted my husband about it, he denied that anything had happened, but I didn't care because, in my mind, the fact that they were talking made him guilty. I was done. I had nothing else left to give. Even though I really struggled with the decision, I knew deep down what I had to do. I prayed, prayed, and prayed some more, but I still felt the same. To me, there was no way I could go on in a marriage in which I had nothing left. I just knew the only way to love freely and be truly happy was to get a divorce. I didn't see any other way. I asked God, *how could I love someone who continues to hurt me?* I didn't have the strength anymore.

I started to mentally prepare myself to move forward with the divorce. I didn't want to leave my home and start all over again, but I wanted and needed to be free from the pain and bondage I felt inside of me. I didn't even feel that God could make my situation better anymore, and I was just done, with a capital D. I felt everything I felt before, but there were no tears. I was simply fed up. I was numb. There was no need in me to cry because crying hadn't gotten me anywhere thus far when it came to infidelity, so I kept my tears.

I told my husband I wanted a divorce. He apologized for what he had done, and got on his knees begging me for another chance. He said if I stayed, I would be the happiest woman in the word. I said no. I didn't have any more chances to give, and neither did I trust anything he said. It was time to move on.

After months of searching, I finally found a place I felt was comfortable for my son and me to live in once we moved out of our home. I found a lawyer, had him draw up papers for an uncontested divorce, and paid my deposit on our new place. I was well on my way to making my life better. I didn't talk to anyone other than the people whose opinions really mattered. I no longer cared what anyone else thought or how they felt; it was all about me and how I felt. I had to care about myself even if no one else did. On top of that, it was my responsibility to protect my son from being hurt, and I didn't want him to grow up in a dysfunctional home where there was no love. He didn't deserve that.

My family helped us move out, and the papers were signed. Even though many things hadn't gone the way I thought they would in my life, I accepted where I was, and I was content. I felt somewhat free because I was finally letting go of it all and starting fresh and making new memories with my son. I was excited about the new life I was going to experience. I had grown older and more experienced, and I was ready for change. I was tired of going around the same mountain; this time, my mountain was going to be moved. I was no longer worried about trusting anyone or being vulnerable with anyone. I had me, myself, and my son, so I was happy. I could count on me not to disappoint me because, after all, I would never hurt myself.

Learning to love yourself first helps you to learn and know your worth.

Months had passed by when I found out my ex-husband had moved on with someone new. I was still single with no one else in sight. I felt angry because, in my mind, how could he love someone when he couldn't even love me the way he was supposed to? I began to feel the same pain I had felt while I was married. I decided that I would go away for the weekend, but really, I wanted to run away and never return to what my life had become.

I dropped my son off with my parents and booked a room in Savannah, Georgia. Once I got there, I walked the block to downtown, checked out the scenery, and went to dinner. I was alone with myself, my thoughts, and my feelings. That night, I couldn't sleep well, so I got up and fell to my knees crying out to God to take the pain away that had resided in me for years; the pain I had held onto because it protected me from ever getting hurt again. I desperately wanted and needed to be free. I thought I had forgiven. I thought I had let it all go. But I hadn't. I was only hurting myself by continuing to hold on to something that only hindered me and stunted my growth.

Early the next morning, after a while of crying out to God, He spoke to me and told me to go to church. I hit the road, speeding and praying that I would make it in time. As I walked into church and made it to my seat, I heard my pastor say, "There is someone here who needs to be delivered and healed from past hurts that are deeply rooted."

By that time, I had lost it. The Lord had touched me in that service and, when I left that day, I was a different woman. I didn't feel heavy anymore. I didn't feel hurt anymore. I felt joy. God showed me myself—how He saw me and what He wanted me to be. That was the day God told me I was healed to help build others. I accepted the purpose on my life, moved forward, and didn't look back. I had finally forgiven from my heart. Why? Because I was ready to let go of what no longer served me so I could truly be free!

More Than a Conqueror

Written by
Elecia James

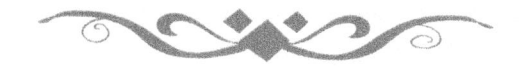

Growing up as a little girl should be fun and exciting. Little girls are usually the apple of their daddy's eye. I definitely was. It is so influential for a father's love to be present to yield a better psychological worth as she grows up, ensuring she does not lack in the development of self-esteem, self-image, or self-respect. She should feel protected, loved, and comforted. When she reaches adulthood, she should walk with her head held high and exude a healthy sense of confidence, security, and dignity.

But what if a father's influence wasn't there? A better question would be, what if a father's influence was there, but another family member's influence was more compelling during the little girl's upbringing? Every only child, no matter their age, wishes to have a loving sibling. In my story, an older half-sister fell into my territory of solace when I was seven years old.

During my childhood years, my biggest fear and weakness was my older sister. We share the same father. He arrived home one day with my half-sister, Daddy's other little girl, in tow. I never asked why she came to live with us. I was just excited about having a big sister! Someone who could share everything with me. But from the moment she moved in with us, her wrath and my nightmare—the abuse—began.

I really thought that she hated me, deep down to her bones. I wanted so desperately for her to love me, but she continuously told me I was ugly and ordered me to repeat her.

Artificial Beauté

I said in a whisper, "I am ugly."

"Good," She said, "Now, say it louder this time like you mean it."

I hesitated as tears welled up in my eyes. *Why is she doing this to me?* And then repeated those words loudly: "I am ugly."

When my cousins came to visit, my dear half-sister called them downstairs to the basement where she had already dragged me minutes prior and lined them up to tell me I was ugly. She pointed to each cousin: "Tell her she's ugly."

One by one, "You are ugly," was uttered from their mouths. Over and over, I heard this statement. So I actually started to believe it. Days with my cousins were so much different when my sister was not around. We'd play and have a good ol' time—that is, until she came in the room. To appease her, my cousins had to straighten up and act like they didn't like me. They were also banned from playing with me.

I endured this harassment and mockery for years, but all I wanted was for her to love me, or at least like me enough to stop. Despite all my begging and pleading to make her stop, it never stopped. It was a part of my life. I didn't exactly accept the abuse—I didn't have a choice. My parents didn't know or suspect. I never told them.

It wasn't that I was an unattractive child. I was a cute little girl, who happened to look just like Daddy but with dimples. My half-sister and I both had beautiful hair; mine was thick and long, but hers was more luscious. I was the darker, chunkier one with dimples, while she was long-legged, light, and thin. She often referred to me as "the dark one." We both wore expensive, gorgeous clothing from the same stores, as my mother was a stickler for being well dressed and conducting yourself as a lady at all times. However, there were times I couldn't locate my clothes, and my wardrobe ended up not being up to par. My sister teased me privately and publicly. This was done on a daily basis.

She also condescendingly expressed that the only thing I knew how to do was play music. But I took that as a compliment. Little did she know, music was my outlet. I would let it take me as far beyond reality as I could go without having to hear the snide tone of her voice plucking at my nerves or threatening to lock me in a dark room, which did happen at times. I existed in my own little world by myself, singing, humming, dancing, or playing the piano, flute, or cello.

At the age of twelve, I was the only little brown face of twenty students who had the opportunity to perform at the iconic Carnegie Hall. I exerted all my frustrations through my music, which resulted in a stellar performance. My parents, my best friend, and a few family members were in attendance. At the conclusion of the concert, my parents were smiling and beaming with pride, while my best friend and other family members rushed up to me, congratulated me, and planted kisses on my cheeks.

Artificial Beauté

My half-sister stood there stone faced. I kind of ignored her and tried to relish in the moment, but then reality hit me—I still had to go home. I sighed heavily and got in the car. As we rounded the corner, I could see my house in the distance through the bushes and trees, and, slowly but surely, my body tensed up. I knew as soon as we were alone in our room, she would be ready to pounce on the abuse-Elecia wagon, so that knocked me right back down into that sick, pit-in-the-stomach feeling.

When she left for college (she was six years older), it was such a relief. But during her holiday breaks, she would return home and pick up where she left off. The abuse, the digs, and the occasional public embarrassment, which included name-calling, always resurfaced.

When I was sixteen, I was selected to sing in performances in Europe for a month. This was huge because only two students from each state were chosen to participate. I thought to myself, *wow, I guess I am good, and I really do have a gift.* For the first time in my life, I was able to look in the mirror and actually say that and believe it. I no longer saw an ugly little girl staring back at me. I smiled. And I was so much prettier after I smiled. I started to hold my head just a little bit higher every day but remained grounded in knowing where my gifts came from.

This invitation extended to me certainly generated an exceptional feeling in my whole being. I felt comfortable and confident. I released my feelings of sadness and anxiety through my music, as singing and playing were my medicine. I even landed a solo during this tour, which was a pleasant surprise.

In my mid-twenties, I had to go home to see my father while he was recovering from his second stroke. Daddy was the love of my life, and this would be a good visit for us. I drove a pleasant four hours from Maryland, but rounding the corner to my childhood home instantly brought a feeling of anxiety. I almost hated going to that house. I felt tense and wound up and sometimes even sick, but I had to check on my daddy.

I walked in and greeted my parents. I sat next to Daddy and tried to relax and chat with him and help him with a few things. I was there for a good twenty minutes when she walked in the door. My half-sister was married with a baby and didn't come around as much, so I had been hopeful that I wouldn't see her during this visit, even though I loved that little baby boy. My heart and all my energy plummeted. I sighed heavily and let my head fall.

It was unusual for the two of us to be home at the same time as adults, so it felt weird. I always made sure she wasn't there when I visited. The drive already hurled me into a weird state, but this definitely soared me into the past, recollecting the bad memories that occurred in this house. Surprisingly, throughout my entire life, my parents hadn't witnessed any of this because she never did it in their presence.

Artificial Beauté

She said, "Hi."

I huffed out a "Hi."

We failed to utter any additional words to one another until she broke the silence and started barking out orders of things that needed to be done around the house. I rolled my eyes and did not budge an inch. Then, she stomped through the room to do what she had demanded me to do.

She nitpicked at my fingernails: "Oh, I see you got your nails done." She neglected to mention that they were a nice color or style; she just turned the corners of her mouth down and nodded. I nodded as well. One would think that when siblings grow up, the ridicule would stay in the past.

Daddy was recovering from his second stroke, and it was a struggle for him to walk, let alone move, and it hurt me to my soul to see him like that. I ran to his aid and held him as we walked together across the room.

My half-sister hollered out, "Let him do it! Why are you helping him? Dad, you're not even trying!" She was a nurse, so it was her job to make sure the patient was able to do it themselves. In this case, it was my father, so I refused to let him struggle.

I hollered back, "Don't yell at him!"

She yelled, "Who are you talking to?"

I yelled at the top of my lungs, "I'm talking to you!"

She looked like a deer in headlights.

Yes, I had finally stood up to her! I felt like the Queen of Zumanda! Ha! Yes! I that moment, I had to protect my dad, so I forgot about how afraid of her I was and just came to his defense. Unfortunately, we upset my dad, and he half yelled "Stop it, Stop it!"

I felt bad for upsetting my daddy, so I apologized to him. I then noticed that I was unusually scratching my head. My hands were shaking. My head was getting hot. I felt myself burning up. My anxiousness began to turn physical and attack me. I had to get out of that house. As usual, that meant walking a few blocks to my best friend Sandra's house. We had known each other since we were eight and could finish each other's sentences. We always shared the good, bad, and ugly.

I stayed at Sandra's house until I calmed down. When I was finally able to breathe, I returned to the house. My sister had left, but then the phone rang. I tensed up as I noticed who was calling my phone. It was her number on the caller ID. Before I could say anything, she said, "You owe me an apology for being so disrespectful."

I let her have it: "You're not going to treat Dad like that; furthermore, you owe me an apology."

I went in on her for a good minute or so before I just hung up, with a smile on my face.

Don't wait for others to validate you. Believe in yourself, you are enough.

To this day, more than forty years after she first came to live with us, I cringe at the sight of her name appearing on my caller ID. I have to take a deep breath and quickly prepare myself to answer the phone. We take turns caring for my mother—her stepmother—so while I battle against my inner being, I cannot ignore her calls, no matter how much I want to. By answering the phone, I can be sure to hear an opinionated rant in a hyperactive tone, advising me how I should feel and act about whatever subject that dominates the conversation. I have to say a prayer for her and myself because sometimes my thoughts are almost evil, which is not how I was raised. Perhaps one day, we'll engage in more positive conversations. Until then, I'm determined to continue to live a positive, stress-free life. I've never asked her why she mistreated and abused me. Once I became an adult, I limited my communication with her, prayed, sought therapy, continued to surround myself with positive people, started believing in myself, and became determined to achieve my goals.

Overcoming abuse, which involves building your self-esteem, is a process, and it can take years to heal, evolve, and handle. Having a support system is an essential part of the healing process. Identify trustworthy, positive individuals who are great listeners and are willing to assist you on this journey. I believe God provided me with my initial support system during my early years: two of my elementary school teachers; my stern piano teacher; my dad, who deposited independence and a goal-oriented "Yes you can" spirit; my mom, who taught me how to be a lady; Granny (Aunt Di), who was always loving and demonstrated extreme kindness toward me and others; and Sandra, my best friend, who was my sounding board and confidant. These were angels sent by Him. Although some of them are no longer with me physically, they remain in a special place in my heart and watch over me in spirit. Not only do I currently have a support system, but I've learned the importance of being a support to others.

Not everyone believes in God, but I do, and I also believe in the power of prayer. To heal, I asked God for help and direction, which then led me to a therapist. I was a little apprehensive at first, but then I decided to take that step. After the first few sessions, I was convinced it was the right decision! Therapy is nothing to be ashamed of. Everyone goes to the doctor for advice and medication to help them get well. It's the same principle. Talking about it and letting your feelings out will equip you with tools to navigate through overwhelming challenges. You are hearing it from a different, professional, impartial source. Don't let fear, stigma, or societal pressure prohibit you from being the "best" you.

Once I applied the strategies I learned and utilized my gifts, I began to reach for the stars with confidence. Each time a door opened and I was able to walk through that door, I'd look up to the sky and say, "Thank you!"

My triumph did not soar until years down the road.

Artificial Beauté

Once an adult, I truly let go. I am a different person today. I am no longer that timid, frustrated little girl who cried daily, had low self-esteem, and had no voice. I'm strong, confident, and determined. I became a voice for the voiceless by advocating for disadvantaged little girls. I've accomplished things beyond my wildest dreams, and I am still striving to do more! You can too! Dream big and believe in yourself! You too can be more than a conqueror! *I can do all things through Christ which strengthens me!*

About the Authors

Bonita Parker is an Inner Beauté Synergist, author, and transformation strategist who is becoming one of the world's most sought-after transformation consultants. Her personal power story highlights the strength it takes to transform from an abandoned child to a successful entrepreneur. She continues to motivate and inspire women worldwide as the visionary behind the *Unmask Yourself Beauté Symposium*, where she speaks to transform lives. To expand her mission and global platform, Bonita launched her digital talk show, "About F.A.C.E. with Bonita Parker," which offers valuable insight on the core challenges women face daily.

Through her authorship and live events, Bonita has made an incredible impact among women and has begun a national trend of *unmasking*. For her noble efforts, she was awarded the Metro Phenomenal

Women's Award in 2015 and the Woman on the Rise Award in 2016.

> To learn more about her initiatives,
> visit www.bparkerenterprises.com

Ida Robinson is a life strategist, motivational speaker, mentor, author, mother of three children, and grandmother of two. A "teen mom" supporter, she is committed to inspiring young moms to dream big and live intentionally. Her own emotionally compelling story of overcoming many obstacles as a former teen mom to becoming a successful six-figure earner has inspired countless young moms to breathe life into their opportunities.

Ida's mission is to encourage young moms to dream bigger and write their vision by offering workshops on education, financial literacy, bridging success, and lifestyle transformation. She motivates and inspires teen moms to live intentionally and to never give up despite their circumstances. Through her initiatives to promote self-love, self-value, and financial independence in her blog *Mom N' Powerment*, she aims to reach women and moms around the globe.

To connect, visit her website at
www.momnpowerment.com

About the Authors

Anne Sewell, founder and CEO of Creative Vision for Women, is a business entrepreneur for a nonprofit, community-based organization that assists at-risk women and teens from various social, economic, and ethnic backgrounds. Anne is a recent graduate of the Steve Harvey School of Business Acceleration 2016, and has been honored with the 2014 Living Legacy Award, 2016 Community Award, and the 2016 ICON Award by *Be There Magazine*.

As a licensed adoptive parent, she has fostered forty-eight kids in her home. After years of experience, research, and work with at-risk kids, Creative Vision for Women announced the birthing of TEENS N2 CREATIVE SUCCESS. Anne's primary goal of focus is to assist troubled women and teens on a path of growth, and to aid them in turning their lives around by realizing they are of extreme importance and they are not alone.

To learn more, visit her website at
www.creativevisionforwomen.com

LuDrean Peterson is the CEO and founder of Delivering On Ideas & Thoughts (DO IT). Her goals are to help others live out their dreams by providing resources and tools so they can overcome hurdles. She serves as a career and business strategist and is passionate about inspiring others to fulfill their dreams, professionally and personally.

LuDrean holds a master of business administration and a master of science in management with an emphasis in human resources management. With over twenty-six years of experience in human resources and sixteen years as an office director and hiring manager, LuDrean specializes in the areas of organizational and career development and is highly skilled in strategizing and advisory services in the workplace. She is highly sought after for mentoring, resume writing, and interview preparation services, and she received the *FDA Pioneer Award* for achieving groundbreaking success.

Learn more at
www.do-it-delivers.com

About the Authors

Kimberly Moorer is the founder and CEO of Heal One Build One, an organization that helps clients heal from their past so they can build one solid foundation in the future. As a certified life coach, author, and motivational speaker, her passion is to empower and inspire individuals to follow their dreams.

To connect, visit her website at
www.healonebuildone.wix.com/coach

Elecia James is a bilingual, multifaceted executive known as "The Girl Ambassador." Originally from White Plains, New York, and born of Jamaican parents, she refers to herself as a "Jamerican." As an educational consultant, dynamic motivational speaker, talented musician, inspirational author, and former principal, Elecia is committed to using her life experiences to empower minority and disadvantaged girls globally. Her career highlights include performing and facilitating workshops, presenting for Dr. Boyce Watkins's "Your Black Education" series, and coproducing *Black Girls Unscripted*, a movement/documentary aimed at inspiring girls and young women of color.

Ms. James was recently appointed as chief of staff for The National Council of Women of America, and her proudest achievement is the development of a mentoring program called Umoja, which focuses on academic achievement and cultural and personal development for low-income youth.

To connect, contact her at
esjmanagement@gmail.com

CREATING DISTINCTIVE BOOKS
WITH INTENTIONAL RESULTS

We're a collaborative group of creative masterminds with a mission to produce high-quality books to position you for monumental success in the marketplace.

Our professional team of writers, editors, designers, and marketing strategists work closely together to ensure that every detail of your book is a clear representation of the message in your writing.

Want to know more?
Write to us at info@publishyourgift.com
or call (888) 949-6228

Discover great books, exclusive offers, and more at
www.PublishYourGift.com

Connect with us on social media

@publishyourgift